DATE DUE		
JAN - 4 '96			
OCT 2 8 '98			
JUN 2 5 '97			
AP 03 '01			
DEC 1 7 2005			
MAR 0 8 2021			

OLD AMERICA

Ghost Towns

Lynn Stone

Rourke Publications, Inc.
Vero Beach, FL 32964

Edited by Sandra A. Robinson

PHOTO CREDITS
© Emil Punter: cover, 18, 19, 21, 22, 26, 27; © Lynn M. Stone: title page, 7, 23, 24; © Robert Pelham: 4, 10; © Noella Ballenger and Jalien Tulley: 6, 8, 13, 15, 16, 17, 28.

Library of Congress Cataloging-in-Publication Data

Stone, Lynn M.
    Ghost towns / by Lynn Stone.
    p. cm. — (Old America)
    Summary: Examines the ghost towns scattered across America, discussing their decline and current status.
    ISBN 0-86625-449-8
    1. Ghost towns – West (U.S.) – Juvenile literature. 2. Ghost towns – Alaska – Juvenile literature. 3. Ghost towns –Yukon Territory – Juvenile literature. 4. West (U.S.) – History, Local – Juvenile literature. 5. Alaska – History, Local – Juvenile literature. 6. Yukon Territory – History, Local – Juvenile literature. [1. Ghost towns.] I. Title. II. Series: Stone, Lynn M. Old America.
F591.S856   1993
978—dc20   93-143
                                                           CIP
                                                            AC
Printed in the USA

TABLE OF CONTENTS

I GHOST TOWNS

True ghost towns are lonely, spooky places.

Where is everyone? Why is this town so deathly quiet? The dusty dirt street is empty. No one peers through the dark windows of tired, gray buildings. No laughter dances on the wind. An owl, up and about in the fading light, passes silently by like a ghost with wings. Wait — a thump! It is just a door, flapping on rusty hinges — or is it? It is becoming as dark as the nearby mountains, too dark to tell. No one turns on a light. *Where is everyone?*

In a ghost town like this, there is no one left to turn on a light. A true ghost town is an entire village or town where no one lives anymore. It is lonely and spooky, filled only with shadows and the secrets of the past. In fact, finding out about a ghost town's past is half the fun of visiting it. Some visitors like to imagine that ghosts of people who lived in the town long ago still haunt the empty buildings and stroll the empty streets. Perhaps they do . . .

The little communities that have become ghost towns were at one time bustling with people. Unlike most North American villages, these towns lost their entire populations. When the people left, a ghost town was born.

Ghost towns survive in various conditions. The most impressive ghost towns are truly **abandoned** — no one lives there. Many of these towns are quite old, often dating back to the late 1800s or early 1900s. They have

The rocky ruins of Clan Alpine, a ghost town in the Nevada hills.

names like Highgrade, Providence, Ingot, Gold Point, Jackrabbit, Silver Reef, Gold Hill, Garnet, Elkhorn, Tomboy, Peerless, Gold Incorporated, Bonanza and Greenhorn. These names help reveal what the town founders had on their minds.

Most ghost towns are in desert regions of the American West, although many others are squirreled away in wooded Western mountains. Towns known as ghost towns may have been actual towns, or they may have been mining camps. Mining camps were little clusters of buildings constructed where miners dug for gold, silver, coal, zinc and other precious metals. True ghost towns also include Native American villages that have been deserted.

Like many other abandoned communities, this crumbling mining camp in Alaska is rapidly disappearing.

A ghost town today, Bodie is part of California's system of state parks.

A partial ghost town is largely abandoned, but it still has a few people living in it. One day it may become a true ghost town, or more people may move there, making the town bubble with activity once again.

Restored ghost towns have been fixed up and preserved. The amount of change and repair that a restored town undergoes varies with each town. Some restored ghost towns look much like they did 100 years ago, but they have stores, hotels and tourist attractions operated by people who live there now. Buildings in the ghost town of Bodie, California, are repaired only when necessary. No one lives in Bodie, and the state of California wants to keep Bodie a true ghost town. Sooner or later, however, every ghost town needs some repair, or it will fall apart and disappear.

A restored ghost town with a clutter of tourists can be a rather busy, noisy place. A deserted town at the end of a bumpy Jeep trail in the desert or on a foggy mountainside is much more ghostly. The moans of wind and old boards are the only sounds there.

II | THE FIRST GHOST TOWNS

The cliff dwellings of early Native Americans are among the oldest ghost towns in North America.

Christopher Columbus "discovered" North America in 1492. When Columbus returned to Europe with news of his discovery, many countries sent ships with explorers and settlers back to North America, the "New World." For 300 years after the first voyage of Columbus, France, Spain and England each staked out sections of North America as its own. Settlers from those nations built villages and towns, many of which have become the modern cities of today. Other towns, abandoned by their builders, became early ghost towns. Nearly all of these have been destroyed over the years by wind, fire, earthquake or neglect. Nothing is left of Jamestown, Virginia, an English settlement established in 1607, except a few brick foundations.

Native people lived in North America long before the European nations knew that North America existed. Like the Europeans who settled here, many of the native people built permanent villages. Some of those villages, in what is now New Mexico, Arizona and Colorado, were abandoned by their owners even before Columbus sailed to North America.

Built of stone and bricklike **adobe**, some of the tribal villages — especially those carved into rocky cliffs — have survived for hundreds of years. They are not perfectly preserved, of course, but some are remarkably fit. Several Native American villages are protected by the U.S. National Park Service for visitors to enjoy. One of the best-known areas of cliff dwellings is Mesa Verde

National Park in Colorado. Hovenweep National Monument in Colorado, Chaco Culture National Historic Park and Gila Cliff Dwellings National Monument, both in New Mexico, also protect ruins of early Native American ghost towns.

III THE MAKING OF A GHOST TOWN

Restored to its old luster, a prospector's church stands in the mountain snow in Bodie, California.

In the second half of the 19th century (1850-1899), Americans pushed westward from the settled lands of eastern North America. What began as a westward trickle of pioneers, explorers and fortune hunters became a flood after the American Civil War ended in 1865. The West held many dangers — hostile Native Americans, rugged mountains, uncharted rivers, bitter cold and broiling heat. Still, open spaces and adventure were powerful lures. Thousands risked danger to travel west.

Among the early settlers of the West were **prospectors**, people who searched for gold, silver and other valuable metals. In 1848 prospectors struck gold in California. It was not the first gold strike, but it was a large strike and drew widespread attention. Because people rushed to the area where gold had been found in the Sierra Mountains, the strike became the first of the great "**gold rushes**." During the next 50 or 60 years, gold and silver rushes occurred from the deserts of New Mexico, to the mountains and streams of Alaska and western Canada.

When word of a gold or silver strike spread, prospectors sometimes arrived by the thousands, pouring into some of the most remote parts of western North America. The fortune hunters needed housing, restaurants, banks, bakeries, saloons, law offices and many other buildings. Gamblers, traders and business people followed the prospectors to the mining sites. Everyone wanted a

Mining towns were not without their problems, and jails were often occupied.

Columbia, California, was deserted when her mines failed, but visitors can relive the old days in the restored town.

piece of the gold pie. Almost overnight, mining camps and new towns arose.

The typical new town did well as long as the mines kept producing gold or silver. Any one area, however, has a limited amount of valuable **ore**, the rock in which metals such as gold and silver are usually found. As the gold and silver ore were mined out of an area, miners left and sought their fortunes and futures somewhere else. Without prospectors to spend money, the town's businesses failed. Suddenly the town had no reason to exist. People streamed away, many of them to a new strike.

Not every ghost town is the result of a mining failure. Towns built to house railroad workers were deserted

When the mines closed in this California ghost town, only the buildings remained.

after the rails were laid. Other towns failed because of floods and fires. Some towns failed for reasons that remain mysteries. The abandonment of Mesa Verde is unexplained, although most scientists think that **drought**, a severe lack of water, forced people to leave that Colorado village.

IV THE WESTERN GHOST TOWNS

Wooden crosses mark the graves of many pioneers who died in towns hundreds of miles from their homes.

The West was as raw and rugged as it was wide. In the second half of the 19th century, towns and mining camps were often tough and lawless. Shootings and stabbings were common. In Bodie, California, a miner wrote, "There's nothing to do but hang around the saloons, get drunk and fight, and lie out in the snow and die." Death in mining towns, however, was not always as peaceful as lying in the snow. During one week in 1879, Bodie buried six men who died in fights.

Gold and silver fever swept through much of the North American West after the California rush faded in the late 1850s. Towns and mining camps sprang up in what are now the states of New Mexico, Arizona, Nevada, Colorado, Utah, Idaho, Oregon, Wyoming,

An old blacksmith's shop in the ghost town of Bland, New Mexico.

Montana, South Dakota, and in British Columbia and Alberta, Canada. For most prospectors, hard work did not result in quick fortune. Dreams — and the towns they built — collapsed as fast as they had risen.

In the desert Southwest, miners and townsfolk struggled with Native Americans, drought, tough ore, bandits and a weak line of supplies. Some of the towns these hardy people built are among the best-preserved of the remaining ghost towns in North America. One of them is Bland, New Mexico, 26 miles southwest of Los Alamos. Bland began life in the 1870s when prospectors found gold and silver there. By 1900 its population had swelled to 3,000. Like other **boom towns**, however, Bland rapidly failed when its gold and silver was mined out. Today Bland is a true ghost town.

Another ghost town gem is the desert village of Cabezon, New Mexico. Cabezon is unique because it preserves old Spanish-style adobe houses, and because it was a farming, rather than mining, community. Lying in the shadow of Cabezon peak, the rocky core of an old volcano, the town of Cabezon was established by Spanish farmers in the late 1700s. This was long before New Mexico was part of the United States.

The Navajo tribe, near Cabezon, viewed the Spanish as intruders. Relations between villagers and Navajos were sometimes violent. However, Cabezon enjoyed nearly 80 years of peace after the U.S. **Cavalry** — soldiers mounted on horses — defeated the Navajos in

One of the finest desert ghost towns, Cabezon, New Mexico, bakes in the desert sun.

1863. The rights of the native people were not taken into account. The village enjoyed peace — but not prosperity.

In later years, Cabezon's farmers traded with the Native Americans. Still, many natives left the area. The lack of trading partners and Cabezon's problems with the Rio Puerco (Puerco River) became overwhelming.

The villagers depended on the river for water, but at times the Rio Puerco was nothing more than a narrow, muddy stream. At other times, the river charged like an angry bull through the little dams the Spanish had built. "*No mas*, no more," said the villagers. In the 1940s the last Spanish villagers left, and Cabezon became a ghost town.

Dry desert air and remote locations have helped many ghost town buildings survive.

Most remaining ghost towns are in the American West, partly because most of the mining activity that created so many of them took place there. Because many Western towns were built in out-of-the-way locations, they have avoided development. Southwestern ghost towns have another survival advantage — dry desert air that reduces damage from moisture.

GHOST TOWNS IN THE FAR NORTH

This log building in a mining camp was built when prospectors poured into the Yukon Territory, Canada, in the 1890s.

Worn and weathered, an old miner's cabin stands in the stillness of the Yukon winter.

Alaska and the Yukon Territory of Canada are dotted with ghost towns. Many of these Northern towns lived and died with the mines. Several ghost towns along the Yukon River were abandoned for another reason. During the first half of the 20th century (1900-1950), the Yukon River was busy with steamboat traffic. The river was a gateway to the roadless North. However, around 1950 the completion of the Alaska Highway and the growing use of airplanes doomed many little river towns.

Mining activity in the Far North peaked during the Klondike Gold Rush of 1897-98. Thousands of prospectors, enduring great hardships, poured into the Yukon

Territory and Alaska. They fought insects, numbing cold, mudslides, mountains, blizzards, bears — and each other. They established dozens of camps that lasted only as long as the gold was mined. While most of the prospectors failed miserably in their search, Alex McDonald reportedly hit a Yukon jackpot. McDonald boasted that he needed 29 mules to haul out the gold he found during just *one* profitable day in 1899. Stories like that kept "gold fever" alive.

A few Northern ghost towns, such as Dyea, Sheep Camp, Upper Labarge and Silver City, survive in various stages of ruin. Others, beaten down by wind and snow, have been reduced to scattered boards and lumps in the ground. Fortunately, tales of life in these Northern frontier towns have fared better than the towns themselves. Just as Mark Twain and Bret Harte retold stories of life in the California mining camps, Jack London and the poet Robert W. Service wrote about the Yukon.

VI GHOST TOWNS TODAY

Artifacts like these old bottles in a Western ghost town have become extremely rare.

In the early part of the 20th century, most North American ghost towns were new, hardly of any interest. Throughout the West, abandoned towns were purposely destroyed, allowed to fall into total ruin, or wrecked by vandals. The towns were also picked over by hunters of **artifacts**, the objects that people made and used in their daily lives, such as bottles and tools. As time passed, the towns that survived became older and less commonplace. They became curiosities. People began to realize that these little towns provided a rare glimpse of America's colorful past.

Dirt roads and mountain passes make the exploration of Western ghost towns a real adventure.

*Ghost towns —
inside and out —
show the scars of
weather and
passing time.*

Several states and organizations have become involved with the preservation of ghost towns. Even so, protection of many towns is left to chance and property owners. Many ghost towns are on private land.

People who plan to visit ghost towns need to remember that some of the finest ghost towns are not open to the public. Plans to visit a privately owned ghost town should be discussed in advance with the owner.

Even ghost towns on public land are not always easy to find. Mountains, canyons and miles of dirt road can make travel to a ghost town almost as much of an adventure today as it was 80 or 90 years ago.

Detailed information about specific ghost towns is available in libraries and from ghost town societies.

The United States Geological Survey publishes maps that show the exact location of many ghost towns.

True ghost towns are worn and weathered. They are towns with no tenants. Their upkeep is managed by wind, snow, sun and rain, not by the helpful splash of paint. Yet even without the glitter, ghost towns are rare and valuable, like the gold that was the lifeblood for many of them.

GLOSSARY

abandoned (uh BAN dund) - to be left without people and care; to be deserted

adobe (uh DOE bee) - a bricklike material made of straw and sun-baked earth

artifact (ART uh fakt) - an object or tool made by people

boom town (BOOM TOWN) - a town undergoing rapid settlement and expansion; a town with sudden growth

cavalry (KAV ul ree) - a group of soldiers mounted on horses

drought (DROWT) - a long period in which water is scarce or unavailable

gold rush (GOLD RUSH) - the rapid movement of people to gold-producing areas

ore (OR) - a hard, natural material that contains a valuable metal, such as silver or gold

prospector (PRAH spek ter) - one who explores an area in search of valuable minerals or metals

restored (re STORD) - renewed, returned to the original condition

INDEX